CW01431653

PORSCHE 911:

THE PRACTICALLY FREE
TRIVIA BOOK

2016 911R

ROBERT MCGOWAN

Also by Robert McGowan

*The International **Best Seller** - Porsche 911:*
The Practically Free Supercar

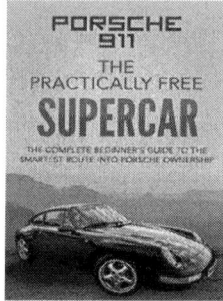

U.K. link http://www.amazon.co.uk/dp/1091444838
U.S. link http://www.amazon.com/dp/1091444838

The International Best Seller - Porsche Boxster:
The Practically Free Sportscar

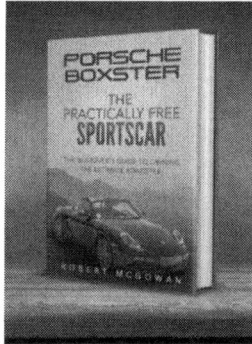

U.K. link http://www.amazon.co.uk/dp/B08GB25HFK
U.S. link http://www.amazon.com/dp/B08GB25HFK

*The International **Best Seller** - Porsche: The Practically Free Coloring Book for Adults and Kids*

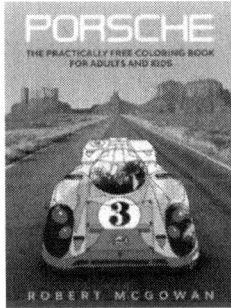

U.K. link http://www.amazon.co.uk/dp/B08L41B432
U.S. link http://www.amazon.com/dp/B08L41B432

Connect with me on my YouTube Channel
And my Free Facebook Group: Practically Free Porsche
https://www.facebook.com/groups/946949849009634

COMING SOON

PORSCHE 911: THE PRACTICALLY FREE TYPE 996

A guide to acquiring and owning the first water-cooled 911

Your Gift

Before we get started, I'd love to offer you a gift. It's my way of saying thank you for spending time with me in this book.

This printable PDF has 108 pages where you can log your miles, fuel, oil, service, maintenance and more to ensure that your Porsche continues to run smoothly. You can ring bind these pages together or keep them in a folder as part of your service records. I'm sure you'll find it very useful.

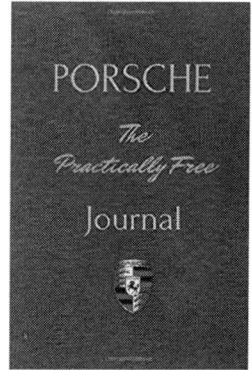

Claim your PDF by clicking the link below and joining my mailing list. Being on my email list means you will be the first to know when I release a new Porsche book, which I plan to offer at a steep discount or free within the first 24 hours.

If you are reading the paperback and would like to access the links then see them on the ebook listing 'look inside' feature.

Download my gift!

Photographs: Robert McGowan, OPC Porsche archives.

As always, members of the Porsche community were extremely kind and helpful. A very special thanks for the photos shared by Jose A Irizarry Selosse, OPC Porsche Stuttgart, the Facebook Porsche Groups and owners' clubs including Practically Free Porsche.

Porsche 911: The Practically Free Trivia Book by Robert McGowan

All rights reserved. The eBook and the paperback contain material protected under International and Federal Copyright Laws and Treaties. Any unauthorized reprint or use of this material is prohibited. No part of this book may be reproduced or transmitted in any form or by any means, electronic or mechanical, including photocopying, recording, or by any information storage and retrieval system without express written permission from the author.

Disclaimer: The opinions within this book are not to be confused with legal or financial advice

© 2021 Robert McGowan

TABLE OF CONTENTS

Introduction

My 993 'Porky' with the Sun setting behind Ben Lomond in the Scottish Highlands

What is it about the Porsche 911 that makes it the most loved and most talked about sportscar in the world? Is it because it's been the benchmark for performance since its introduction in 1964? Is it because of its motorsport heritage or its reputation for toughness and reliability? Perhaps it's simply because it tugs at your heart strings every single time you look at – or it might be how it makes you feel each time you drive it?

The truth is that it's all these things and more. Much more. The 911 is special and unique. It stirs your soul like nothing else can. For many it's the car that they first fell in love with when they were a kid and have dreamed about owning ever since.

Some people clearly remember the feeling of seeing and hearing a 911 Turbo for the first time as it raced passed them on the road. Others talk about being mesmerized by the Porsche commercials and the movies that featured 911s. These experiences give birth to a passion and desire that lasts a lifetime.

Although it has evolved many times over the years you can still see the direct lineage between the first 911's and the latest cars. It has a timeless and enduring appeal that has won the hearts and minds of generations of adoring fans.

This trivia book is for those fans and anyone else who has an interest in all things Porsche. It is intended as a fun way to learn some of the most intriguing insights and the less known facts about the legendary Porsche 911.

There's something in this book for everyone, whether you are completely new to Porsche or a hardcore enthusiast. This quiz is the perfect way to test both yours and your friends 911 knowledge. You'll enjoy giving the answers that you think you know and you'll have fun guessing the ones that you don't.

Plus, you will learn some fascinating insights along the way.

Are you ready for the challenge?

Inside this quizbook you will find over 230 questions ranging between multiple choice and true or false questions. The answers are shown at the end of each chapter and where an answer is false the correct answer is given.

We will go back in time to when the Porsche company started and track the 911 and its evolution through the years. You will learn all about the model types, the numerous triumphs and victories, key statistics, sales, the key players and more. By the end of this book you will be an accomplished 911 expert!

One more thing I feel I should mention. If you are new to my 'Practically Free Porsche' book series you may be wondering why I named it so. Porsches aren't free right? No, clearly, they're not. Can Porsche ownership be practically free motoring? If you buy the right car at the right price then the answer is yes absolutely.

In my best-selling Porsche books and audiobooks, I share my personal experience on exactly how I have enjoyed practically free motoring over three Porsches since 2007. If you want to learn more then check them out for yourself. I think you will get real value and inspiration from them.

Finally, thank you for buying this little quizbook. I had a lot fun writing it and I really do hope you enjoy it. Now let's get started.

Robert McGowan

Chapter 1: 30 Questions

HOW IT ALL STARTED

Ferdinand Porsche at the wheel of a petrol-electric hybrid that he designed.

1. What was the name of the first hybrid electric vehicle built by Ferdinand Porsche in 1899?

a. The Lohner-Porsche Mixte Hybrid
b. The P1
c. The Type 1
d. The Butzi

2. The first contract for the new Porsche Construction Office in 1931 came from the Auto Union under its Wanderer brand. It was a 2-liter, 6-cylinder vehicle which would become known as the Porsche Type

a. 7
b. 1
c. 9
d. 101

3. Hitlers Porsche commissioned Volkswagen (Peoples Car) project was to be available to all citizens of the Third Reich for the equivalent of

a. $396
b. $1934
c. $911
d. $599

4. The early 356s body panels made in Gmund were handcrafted from

a. Mild Steel
b. Aluminum
c. Titanium
d. Steel Alloy

5. 'Dr. Ing. hc' stands for 'Doktor Ingeniuer Honoris Causa'

a. True
b. False

6. Ferdinand Porsche joined the Daimler Corporation in 1905

a. True
b. False

7. What month in 1931 was Porsche officially founded?

a. April
b. May
c. June
d. July

8. How many syllables does the word Porsche have?

a.1
b.2
c.3
d.4

9. Ferdinand Porsche was accused of war crimes and did time in a French prison.

a. True
b. False

10. Porsche used a horizontally opposed "boxer" engine because its flat and compact with a low center of gravity. Who first designed a flat engine?

a. Hans Mezger
b. Ferdinand Porsche
c. Carl Benz
d. Walter Rohrl

11. The 911 was the successor of the 356C. The final ten 356C automobiles produced in March 1966 were convertibles made specifically for which Police Force?

a. US
b. German
c. Dutch
d. Austrian

12. Porsche presented the new type 901 at the IAA in Frankfurt in September 1963. Which car manufacturer objected to any model designation with a zero in the middle?

a. Citroen
b. Peugeot
c. Maserati
d. Ferrari

13. Porsche renamed the 901 as the 911. How many 901's were made before the name change?

a. 82
b. 901
c. 911
d. 63

14. The first 911's horizontal 2 liter flat six engine put out

a. 115 bhp
b. 120 bhp
c. 125 bhp
d 130 bhp

15. The first production car to bear the Porsche name was a type

a. 64
b. 550
c. 356
d. 365

16. The history of the Porsche brand as we know it begins in?

a.1938
b.1939
c.1944
d.1948

17. In which city was the first branded Porsche car approved?

a. Stuttgart
b. Berlin
c. Kärnten
d. Salzburg

18. The first branded production Porsche had a modified 1.1L Volkswagen Beetle engine which put out

a. 35 bhp

b. 55 bhp

c. 85 bhp

d. 105 bhp

19. Porsche were forced to use parts from the Beetle due to shortages

a. True

b. False

20. What was the name of the very first Porsche built in 1939

a. Type 39

b. Type 63

c. Type 64

d. Walter

21. The antlers along with the red and black stripes on the Porsche emblem come from which German state?

a. Hamburg

b. Berlin

c. Baden Württemberg

d. Bremen

22. Who designed the original 911?

a. Ferdinand Porsche
b. Ferdinand Alexander Porsche
c. Pinky Lai
d. Erwin Komenda

23. Ferry Porsches son Ferdinand (Butzi) Porsche penned the original 4 seated designs which would later develop into the 911. 7 prototypes were built. They were called the

a. 901 T1
b. 694 T6
c. 754 T7
d. 745 T7

24. How many short wheel base 911s were produced between 1964 and 1968

a. 1964
b. 5,911
c. 6,607
d. 9,901

25. The 911s distinctive roofline was developed using elements of aircraft aerodynamics. Which term entered in the dictionary in 1970 describes the

gradually sloping roof from the windshield to the rear edge?

a. Sloper
b. Liftback
c. Fastback
d. Kammback

26. When were the first 911s exported to the US?

a. November 1964
b. December 1964
c. January 1965
d. February 1965

27. How much did the first 911 cost in the US?

a. $3500
b. $4500
c. $5500
d. $6500

28. The name 901 was originally chosen because

a. It was the 901st design project to leave the Porsche works since the beginning
b. The 356 had taken part in 901 events
c. It sounded and looked right
d. It could be easily remembered

29. Which City are Porsche HQ located?

a. Berlin
b. Stuttgart
c. Hamburg
d. Munich

30. Which automotive manufacturing company owns Porsche?

a. Mercedes Benz
b. Volkswagen
c. BMW
d. Bugatti

Chapter 1: AnsweRS

1. a. The Lohner-Porsche Mixte Hybrid
2. a. 7
3. a. $396
4. b. Aluminum
5. a. True
6. False it was 1906
7. a. April
8. b.2
9. a. True
10. Benz
11. c. Dutch
12. b. Peugeot
13. a.82
14. d 130 bhp
15. c. 356
16. d.1948
17. c. Kärnten
18. a. 35 bhp
19. a. True
20. c. Type 64
21. c. Baden Württemberg
22. b. Ferdinand Alexander Porsche

23. c. 754 T7
24. c. 6,607
25. c. Fastback
26. d. February 1965
27. c. $5500
28. a. It was the 901st design project to leave the Porsche works since the beginning
29. b. Stuttgart
30. b. Volkswagen

Fast facts

- Ferdinand Porsche was conscripted in 1902 where he served as a chauffeur to Archduke Franz Ferdinand of Austria.

- Ferdinand Porsche developed a car at Austro-Daimler named 'Sacha' after its film maker owner. Sacha was much smaller than its competition and went on to win 43 races including the Targa Florio in 1922.

- Ferdinand designed the Mercedes- Benz type 80 in 1939. With a top speed of 470 mph, it was intended to be the fastest car on Earth. It never ran due to Global events at the time.

- The very first Beatle was built in Ferdinand's private villa.

- Ferdinand Porsche designed the Porsche logo on a napkin as he sat across from US importer Max Hoffman.

Chapter 2: 60 Questions

MODELS

911 type 964; front: 911 Carrera 4 3.6 Cabriolet; Center: 911 Carrera 4 3.6 Targa; rear: 911 Carrera 4 3.6 Coupé 1990

1. What does the 'RS' stand for on the 1973 911 2.7 RS?

a. Rallye Sport
b. Racing Series
c. Rennsport
a. Refined and Sporting

2. The 1965 911 is 11 inches shorter and 9 inches narrower than a 2021 type 992

a. True
b. False

3. The 912 was originally designed to replace the 911

a. True
b. False

4. The 1973 911 Carrera RS had a retractable rear spoiler called a ducktail

a. True
b. False

5. The original RS Ducktail inspired rear spoiler was also known as the

a. Wurzel
b. Burzel
c. Shcnurzel
d. Murzel

6. The 911 Carrera 3.0 RS and the first 911 Turbo both had a whale tale rear spoiler.

a. True

b. False

7. The 1984 911 type 930 had a new tea tray rear spoiler designed to accommodate the intercooler for the updated forced induction flat 6.

a. True

b. False

8. The aborted 4 door 911 project was called the

a. 984

b. 898

c. 989

d. 907

9. The tea tray spoiler was used in the 964 Turbo 3.3 and 3.6 however the 964 Turbo S and the RS America reverted back to the whale tail style as used in the 1970s.

a. True

b. False

10. The 964 RS 3.8 was the first production 911 to be fitted with a single plane wing supported by two swept backend plates

a. True
b. False

11. Which 911 first featured 4-wheel drive?

a. 930
b. 964
c. 993
d. 996 C4S

12.The 992 GT3 RS has the largest non turbo engine ever fitted to a production 911

a. True
b. False

13. The 991 911R has the same engine as which model?

a. 991 Turbo
b. 911 GTS
C. 991 GT3RS
d. 991 Cup car

14. The Porsche Diesel Super manufactured between 1956 and 1963 is what type of vehicle?

a. Motorcycle
b. Tractor
c. Aircraft
d. Soft top sports car

15. What years was the 959 available for sale?

a. 1984-1991
b. 1985-1992
c. 1987-1989
d. 1986-1989

16. Which Porsche model did James Dean die in?

a. 550 Spyder
b. 718 RSK
c. 356C
d. 911 Turbo

17. The 1997 911 Turbo S has more horsepower than a 2008 Porsche Cayenne Turbo S.

a. True
b. False

18. Which model was not sold in the 90's?

a. 930
b. 964
c. 993
d 944

19. Which has the fastest 0-60 time?

a. 2004 911 GT3
b.2011 Panamera Turbo
c. 1987 911 Turbo
d. 2013 Boxster S PDK

20. Only 25 of the original 911R's were made. 20 Vehicles plus 5 test cars

a. True
b. False

21. What is the MSRP for a 2014 Porsche 918 Spyder?

a. $876,000
b. $854,000
c. $845,000
d. $858,000

22. Which is NOT a Porsche racing model?

a. 936
b. 996
c. 908
d. 961

23. What engine size does the 1996 911 GT1 Strassenversion have?

a. 6.3 10-Cylinder
b. 5.4 8-Cylinder
c. 3.2 6-Cylinder
d. 3.6 6-Cylinder

24. How many 959's in total were made?

a. 331
b. 959
c. 337
d. 550

25. Which car built from a 911 was the fastest production car from 1987-1993 and held the fastest time at the Nordschleife?

a. Singer
b. RUF CTR
c. RUF RS
d. 911 Speedster

26. What does Macan translate as?

a. A type of nut
b. A Tiger
c. An ancient Mexican Tribe
d. The act of not returning borrowed books

27. Name the Porsche prototype family car designed for the Chinese market in 1994?

a. The C100
b. The Schietzmobile
c. The C88
d. The C2000

28. What year did Porsche introduce the first 911 Turbo?

a. 1975
b. 1977

29. The first 911 convertible appeared as a 1983 MY

a. True
b. False

30. What year did Porsche switch from air cooled to water cooled 911 engines?

a.1989

b.1997

c.1999

d.2000

31. What is the name of the road biased version of the 2.7 RS?

a. Rennsport

b. Campaign model

c. Touring

d. GTS

32. What is the rarest Porsche 911 based model?

a. Porsche 935 'Street'

b. 993 speedster

c. 911 CSR

d. 959 Komfort

33. The 959 was illegal in the US until 1999 because-

a. It was deemed too fast for the road

b. Porsche did not supply 4 cars for crash testing therefore the car was never certified by the NHTSA

c. The Show or Display Law deemed it unsafe for street use

d. A catalytic converter and reprogrammed computer was not available for the 959 prior to 1999

34. The first 911's in 1964 had a 2-litre flat six engine which put out

a. 125 bhp
b. 130 bhp
c. 135 bhp
d. 140 bhp

35. The more powerful 911S with 160 bhp was introduced in

a. 1965
b. 1966
c. 1967
d. 1968

36. The 911S engine was developed and fitted to the mid-engine 904 and 906 with an increase in power to 210 then later 220 bhp

a. True
b. False

37. The 911A series with its dual brake circuits and 5.5J-15 widened wheels went into production in

a. January 1967
b. March 1967
c. August 1967
d. November 1967

38. The first 911 Targa had a new toughened safety glass rear screen

a. True
b. False

39. The 996 and 997 Targa had a glass rear hatch which could be opened

a. True
b. False

40. Which generation of 911 Targa had a complete makeover which included an electric version of the classic Targa roll bar design?

a. Fourth
b. Fifth
c. Sixth
d. Seventh

41. The 992 Targa 4S has a twin Turbo flat six which has a top speed of 189 mph. How fast can it get to 62 mph?

a. 3.5 seconds
b. 3.6 seconds
c. 3.7 seconds
d. 3.8 seconds

42. The 991 Targa 4 (7 speed manual) weighs

a. 1540 kg
b. 1634 kg
c. 1491 kg
d. 1390 kg

43. Launched in 1967 the 911T had

a. 110 bhp
b. 120 bhp
c. 130 bhp
d. 140 bhp

44. The original 911T replaced the

a. 911S
b. 911E
c. 912
d. 911A

45. The 1967 911R is the lightest 911 constructed by the factory to date

a. True
b. False

46. With its glass fiber bonnet, doors and wings and plexiglass the 1967 911R weighed

a. 1300kg
b. 1150kg
c. 900kg
d. 800kg

47. In the 911R the 'R' stands for

a. Rennsport
b. Rally
c. Race
d. Road

48. The semi-automatic clutch less 911 Sportomatic was introduced in 1969

a. True
b. False

49. The 911 B series went into production in August 1968

a. True
b. False

50. In 1969 the wheelbase was lengthened for 911 and 912 models from 87 to 89.3 inches to help with instability at high speed

a. True
b. False

51. What model year were the 2.4 liter 911's?

a. 1969-1970
b. 1971-1972
c. 1972-1973
d. 1973-1974

52. What was the name of the newer stronger transmission on the 2.4-liter 911s?

a. 901
b. 915
c. G50
d. 950

53. Which series of 911 was known as the 'Olklappe' meaning '4th' door because of its extra oil filler / inspection flap?

a. 911 A
b. 911 B
c. 911 E
d. 911 G

54. Which series of 911 had the oil tank replaced back to its original position because gas station attendants often filled gasoline into the oil tank?

a. 911 E
b. 911 B
c. 911 F
d. 911 A

55. Impact bumpers were designed to withstand a collision at 8 mph without damage will driving forward or reversing

a. True
b. False

56. The G series 911's were made from

a. Model Year 1974 (Aug 73 to July 74 production)
b. Model Years 1974-1989
c. Model Year 1976 (Aug 75 to July 76 production)
d. Model Year 1977 (Aug 76 to July 77 production)

57. The first 911 Turbo was named 930 because Ernst Fuhrmann adapted turbo technology and applied it to the 3.0 liter flat six used in the Carrera RS 3.0

a. True
b. False

58. The 911 from 1978-1983 is known as the

a. Carrera SC
b. 911 Carrera SC
c. 911 SC
d. SC

59. SC stands for Super Carrera

a. True

b. False

60. The 1982 911 Convertible was the first Porsche cabriolet since the 356 in the mid sixties

a. True

b. False

Chapter 2: AnsweRS

1. c. Rennsport
2. a. True
3. b. False it was made as a cheaper alternative to the 911
4. b. False – The ducktail wasn't retractable
5. b. Burzel
6. a. True
7. a. True
8. c.989
9. a. True
10. a. True
11. b. 964
12. a. True
13. C. 991 GT3RS
14. b. Tractor
15. d. 1986-1989
16. a. 550 Spyder
17. b. False the 1997 911 Turbo S has 424 bhp whereas the 2008 Porsche Cayenne Turbo S has 542 bhp
18. a. 930
19. b. 2011 Panamera Turbo

20. b. False. 23 were made. 19 vehicles plus 4 test cars.
21. c. $845,000
22. b. 996
23. c. 3.2 6-Cylinder
24. c. 337
25. b. RUF CTR
26. b. A Tiger
27. c. The C88
28. a. 1975
29. a. True
30. b.1997
31. c. Touring
32. a. Porsche 935 'Street'
33. b. Porsche did not supply 4 cars for crash testing therefore the car was never certified by the NHTSA
34. b. 130 bhp
35. b. 1966
36. a. True
37. c. August 1967
38. b. False it had a removable plastic rear screen
39. a. True
40. d. Seventh

41. d. 3.8 seconds
42. a.1540 kg
43. a. 110 bhp
44. c. 912
45. a. True
46. d. 800kg
47. c. Race
48. b. False it was released in1967
49. a. True
50. a. True
51. c. 1972-1973
52. b. 915
53. c. 911 E
54. c. 911 F
55. False – it was 8 km (or 5 mph)
56. b. Model Years from 1974-1989
57. a. True
58. c. 911 SC
59. a. True
60. a. True

Fast facts

- The first 356 prototype 356/1 had its engine in the middle, not the rear.

- The 911 GT1 the 911 RSR 19 all have mid-mounted engines.

- Most of the early Porsche cars were actually made from bodies from Reutter Carrosserie Werke. When Porsche bought the body making part of the company the remaining company was renamed Recaro.

- Porsche developed the PFM 3200 aircraft engine from the air-cooled flat six used in the 911.

- Porsche designed a gasoline powered Tractor for coffee farmers so that diesel fumes wouldn't impact upon the flavor.

- The all-wheel drive 959 was the technologically advanced supercar of its time. It won its class at the 24 hours of Le Mans and it won the Paris Dakar Rally

Chapter 3: 24 Questions

GIVING SHAPE TO DREAMS

911 Turbo S Design Sketch

1. Which car manufacturer introduced its 'just in time' process to Porsche during the 90's which revolutionized the way all Porsches were made?

e. Mazda

f. Nissan

g. Volkswagen

h. Toyota

2. 'Carrera' means what in Spanish?

a. A sporty motor vehicle
b. High Performance
c. Race
d. Endurance event

3. What does PCCB stand for?

a. Porsche Country Club Board
b. Porsche Carbon Composite Body
c. Porsche Ceramic Cooling Bearing
d. Porsche Ceramic Composite Brake

4. 'Carrara White' is a popular Porsche color (Carrara is spelt correctly 😊)

a. True
b. False

5. The 911 type 996 and the Boxster type 986 share identical front two thirds

a. True
b. False

6. Porsche impact bumpers were introduced in response to new bumper regulations in the US in 1972. The new legislation was intended to

a. Improve safety
b. Reduce repair costs in the event of a low-speed accident

7. What was the launch color of the 911 Turbo S Exclusive Series?

a. Lime Gold Metallic
b. Peridot Green
c. Golden Yellow Metallic
d. GT Silver Metallic

8. The first forged aluminum alloy Fuchs wheels were fitted to a 911 Targa presented at the 1965 IAA auto show to gauge response to the revolutionary wheel design.

a. True
b. False

9. OTTO Fuchs forging process resulted in wheels that were 5kg each which was _____kg lighter than the standard 911 steel wheels at the time

a. 1kg
b. 2kg
c. 3kg
d. 4kg

10. Porsche partnered with Fuchs due to their experience of lightweight materials in the aerospace sector

a. True
b. False

11. Porsche wanted lightweight alloy wheels because

a. They look good
b. They were cheaper to mass produce
c. The effect that unsprung mass has on handling and chassis dynamics
d. Porsche wanted to use a specific tire on the new model

12. The 1967 911S was the first car to sport the Fuchs wheel design after Porsche ordered 5000 wheels from OTTO Fuchs

a. True
b. False

13. The word Targa was used because Porsche had enjoyed success in the Targa Florio race. What does Targa mean in Italian?

a. Roofless
b. Sharp edged
c. Number plate
d. Victory

14. Porsche partnered with Fuchs due to their experience of lightweight materials in the aerospace sector

a. True
b. False

15. What was the name on the standard wheels on the 964 until they were changed in 1992?

a. Design 911
b. Cup 2
c. Fusch Pro
d. Design 90

16. Porsche have patented seat mounted wind deflectors to avoid the wind messing your hair

a. True
b. False

17. Porsche Design developed the world's first black chronograph watch in 1972

a. True
b. False

18. Impact bumpers were used on all production 911s from
a. 1974-1989
b. 1976-1987
c. 1978-1989
d. 1979-1988

19. The 930S 'slant nose' had torpedo shaped front wings and had pop up headlights.

a. True
b. False

20. In 1979 Porsche intended to discontinue the 911 in favor of the

a. 924
b. 944 Turbo
c. 928
d. 968 CS

21. Although the SC and Carrera 3.2 are almost identical looking. The 1984 Carrera differs in that it has

a. A different steering wheel
b. Twin exhaust
c. A redesigned dashboard with larger AC vents
d. New design sports seats

22. Why did the whale tail and tea tray spoiler have rubber edges?

a. To protect pedestrians
b. For added aerodynamics
c. It was cheaper to manufacture
d. For atheistic reasons

23. The M491 option offered in 1984 was known in the UK as the

a. Turbo look
b. SSEE
c. Widebody CS
d. RS

24. The special edition 964 RS offered 4 factory options including a LSD, Stereo, AC and Sunroof and was available in

a. 1990
b. 1991
c. 1992
d. 1993

25. The 993's multi-link rear suspension was taken from the 959

a. True
b. False

26. How many units of the soft rear window, short wheelbase Targa with the S engine were produced between 1966 and 1968?

a. 911
b. 920
c. 925
d. 930

27. In 1967 new 911s came with what coating on the chassis?

a. Powder Coating
b. Waxoyl
c. 2 coats of grey primer
d. 2 component black paint

28. In order create a true classic, Porsche designers always strive for a shape which is modern but never fashionable

a. True
b. False

29. What does the 'G' stand for in Porsches G type gearboxes?

a. Getgag
b. Getrag
c. Gertag
d. Getgo

30. The last 911 to feature floor hinged pedals is the

a. 964
b. 993
c. 996
d. 997 GT3 RS

Chapter 3: AnsweRS

1. d. Toyota
2. c. Race
3. d. Porsche Ceramic Composite Brake
4. a. True
5. a. True
6. b. Reduce repair costs in the event of a low-speed accident
7. c. Golden Yellow Metallic
8. a. True
9. c. 3kg
10. a. True
11. c. The effect that unsprung mass has on handling and chassis dynamics
12. a. True
13. c. Number plate
14. a. True
15. d. Design 90
16. a. True
17. a. True
18. a. 1974-1989

19. b. False. It has pop up headlights but the front wings are flat like the Porsche935 racecar
20. c. 928
21. c. A redesigned dashboard with larger AC vents
22. a. To protect pedestrians
23. a. Turbo look
24. b. 1991
25. b. False it was taken from the stillborn Porsche 989
26. c. 925
27. d. 2 component black paint
28. a. True
29. b. Getrag
30. b. 993

Fast facts

- Porsche designed a 60-degree overhead cam engine for Harley Davidsons racing division.

- The Porsche Design Tower in Miami features robotic elevators and carousels that deliver cars to apartments.

- Porsche designed a state-of-the-art grill with infra-red technology instead of charcoal or gas. It was dubbed the X -Series 2.

- All 911s are manufactured in one place. The Porsche factory in Stuttgart. The factory currently produces 110 911s daily.

- Each 911 has around 5,000 welds

Chapter 4: 25 Questions

KEY PLAYERS

*Ferry Porsche in his office with son
Ferdinand Alexander Porsche 1960*

1. The 917 was designed by Hans Mezger under the supervision of

a. Ferdinand Alexander Porsche
b. Ferdinand Piech
c. Gerhard Mitter
d. Hans Frei

2. Butzi Porsche was born in Stuttgart on Dec 23rd 1935

a. True

b. False

3. Porsche racing driver Hans Herman had 14 participations to his credit in the 24 Hours of Le Mans. He was also a trained

a. Basket Weaver

b. French Polisher

c. Baker

d. Plumber

4. Ferdinand Alexander Porsche founded the Porsche Design Studio in

a. 1971

b. 1972

c. 1973

d. 1974

5. Erwin Komenda was a major contributor to the bodywork design of several significant Porsche sportscars

a. True

b. False

6. In 1976 Jacky Ickx and his team mates claimed the first 24 Hours of Le Mans victory for a turbo charged engine in a

a. 911
b. 935
c. 917
d. 936

7. Norbert Singer worked as chief crash tester at Porsche throughout his career.

a. True
b. False

8. Fritz Enzinger and Andreas Seidl are both credited as the 'workhorses' of Porsches LMP1 programme between 2014 and 217

a. True
b. False

9. Credited with saving Porsche from bankruptcy Wendelin Wiedeking was Chief Executive Officer at Porsche from

a. 1993 to 2009
b. 1995 to 1997
c. 1999 to 2003
d. 2004 to 2007

10. Ferdinand (Ferry) Porsche and Dorothy Reitz's youngest son is called

a. Ferdinand Junior Porsche
b. Butzi
c. Big Franco
d. Wolfgang Heinz Porsche

11. Who was the Chief Engineer at Porsche who amongst other notable things was responsible for designing the 911 air-cooled engines?

a. Hans Mezger
b. Harm Lagaay
c. Ferdinand Alexander Porsche
d. Michael Mauer

12. The 'Porsche' name originates from the German word 'Bursche' which means 'boy, young man, apprentice, farmhand'

a. True
b. False

13. Who designed the 911 type 996 and the tandem built Boxster type 986?

a. Pinky Lai
b. Anton Piech
c. Reutter
d. Karman

14. Which CEO at Porsche decided to continue with the 911 despite calls to replace it

a. Peter Schutz
b. Oliver Blume
c. Wolfgang Porsche
d. Abuzar Bokhari

15. Porsche motorsport driver Walter Rohrls first Porsche was a _____

a. 944 Turbo
b. 930
c. 356 B
d. 924 Carrera GT

16. Which Porsche CEO said 'the 911 will be the last Porsche which is going for full electrification?'

a. Anton Piech
b. Ferry Porsche
c. Oliver Blume
d. Martin Winterkorn

17. Hans Deiter Potsche became Chairman of the Board at Volkswagen following the resignation of Ferdinand Piech

a. True
b. False

18. Ferdinand Karl Piech was Ferdinand Porsches great grandson

a. True
b. False

19. Ferdinand Piech influenced the design of the 911, the Audi Quattro and the Bugatti Veyron

a. True
b. False

20. At the time of writing Hiltrude Werner is the sole woman on Volkswagen AG's Board of Management

a. True
b. False

21. Racing legend Stirling Moss owned a Porsche _____

a. 718 RS 61 Spyder
b. 817 RS 61 Spyder
c. 781 RS 61 Spyder
d. 761 RS 71 Spyder

22. Which cars fuel system did Norbert Singer work on his 2nd day at Porsche?

a. 962
b. 917
c. 911
d. 356C

23. Which of these two statements is true? Porsche CEO Arno Bohn

a. wrote a letter to Ferdinand Piech suggesting that he resign from the Porsche Supervisory Board
b. presided over the 944 developments

24. Who is the first female Porsche works driver?

a. Simone Smith
b. Simona de Silvestro
c. Simona Le Bon
d. Simona Garfunkel

25. Who set a lap record of 5:19:55 round the Nürburgring in a Porsche 919 Hybrid Evo?

a. Walter Rohl
b. Timo Bernhard
c. Stefan Bellof
d. Jordan Belfort

Chapter 4: AnsweRS

1. e. Ferdinand Piech
2. b. False – it was Dec 11th
3. c. Baker
4. b. 1972
5. a. True
6. d. 936
7. b. False - he worked as Project Manager for most of Porsches racing cars
8. a. True
9. a. 1993 – 2009
10. d. Wolfgang Heinz Porsche
11. a. Hans Mezger
12. a. True
13. a. Pinky Lai
14. a. Peter Schutz
15. c. 365 B
16. c. Oliver Blume
17. a. True
18. b. False – he was his grandson
19. a. True
20. a. True
21. a. 718 RS 61 Spyder

22. b. 917
23. a. Wrote a letter to Ferdinand Piech suggesting that he resign from the Porsche Supervisory Board
24. b. Simona de Silvestro
25. c. Stefan Bellof

Fast facts

- Black, Red, and White are the most popular Porsche colors.

- 15% of the Porsche factory's workforce is female.

- It is estimated that 2 thirds of 911s built since the beginning are still on the road today.

- Parts taken from the wreck of James Deans ill-fated 550 Spyder were used in other cars. All of which ended up in an accident of its own.

- 911s require more pressure in the rear tires to its rear weight bias.

- 911s have A symmetrical door mirrors

Chapter 5: 20 Questions

SALES

*First Porsche factory collection by a customer on
May 26th 1950 in Zuffenhausen*

1. Where is the largest Porsche market in terms of volume?

a. US

b. China

c. Germany

d. UK

2. Who is largest Porsche dealer in the US?

a. Wild Turkey Porsche
b. Single Malt Porsche
c. Jack Daniels Porsche
d. Gin and Tonic Porsche

3. How many OPCs are in the UK at the time of writing?

a. 39
b. 43
c. 45
d. 47

4. In 1980 Porsche withdrew the 930 from the US and Chinese markets (although it remained for sale in Canada) due to

a. Safety concerns because of accidents caused by snap oversteer
b. Changing emissions regulations
c. Low sales
d. The oil crisis

5. Despite the factory closing for a period during the C19 pandemic Porsches global sales dipped by only

a. 3%
b. 4%
c. 10%
d. 17.5%

6. Which of these 911s are the rarest in terms of build numbers?

a. 997 C4S
b. 993 Carrera
c. 997 Carrera S
d. 996 Carrera

7. Which of these 911s had the most sales?

a. 997 Carrera S
b. 996 Carrera
c. 911 SC
d. 911 Carrera 3.2

8. Although production of the 959 ended in 1986 an additional six 959 Komforts were built in 1992

a. True
b. False

9. 991 Targa 4S Heritage Editions were made

a. True
b. False

10. The 911 is Porsches best-selling model consistently

a. True
b. False

11. How many 996 GT3 RS were made?

a. 690
b. 680
c. 996
d. 911

12.How many 996 GT3 RS were sent to UK?

a. 120
b. 220.
c. 320
d. 430

13. The 991 Speedster was developed from the 2016 911 R and the GT3 and only 1948 were made

a. True
b. False

14. A 1995 993 GT2 sold at auction for
_____in September 2016

a. £1.8 M
b. £1.2 M
c. £960 K
d. £945 K

15. A 1998 911 Strassenversion sold at auction in for just under £4 M

a. True
b. False

16. How many 911 Strassenversions were made?

a. 10
b. 20
c. 30
d. 40

17. How many 964 RS were made?

a. 2, 276
b. 2, 275
c. 2, 274
d. 2, 273

18. In the limited run 997 SC. 'SC' stands for

a. Super Carrera
b. Super Classic
c. Sport Classic
d. Sport Carrera

19. Upon its launch the first 911 Targa had much stronger than expected. Demand quickly outstripped supply making them highly sought after

a. True
b. False

20. Porsche produced the 1000th 911 2.7 RS in 1973 on

a. April 1st
b. April 7th
c. April 9th
d. April 13th

Chapter 5: AnsweRS

1. b. China
2. c. Jack Daniels Porsche
3. c. 45
4. b. Changing emissions regulations
5. a. 3%
6. a. 997 C4S (30, 973)
7. d. 911 Carrera 3.2 70, 044
8. a. True
9. b. False – 992 were made
10. b. False the Macan and Cayenne currently outsell it
11. b. 680
12. a. 120
13. a. True
14. a. £1.8 M
15. a. True
16. b. 20
17. a. 2, 276
18. c. Sport Classic
19. b. False – they weren't initially successful
20. c. April 9th

Fast facts

- The prancing horse on the Porsche crest is similar to Ferraris. Porsche used it because of the link with horse breeding in Stuttgart as shown on its coat of arms. Ferrari used the horse logo partly because an Italian fighter pilot was shot down over Stuttgart in WW1.

- On left hand drive 911s the ignition is on the left partly because it made it quicker to insert the key during running starts at Le Mans and also because it saved a small amount of money and weight by having less wiring.

- The 911 type 992 almost had air suspension but the idea was dropped due to its weight implications. Porsche already had a 911 prototype from the early 80s with air suspension.

- The first 25 type 917s were built by secretaries along with other personnel in order to quickly make the car race legal. As such it was nicknamed 'secretary car'.

- The Airbus A300 cockpit was designed by Porsche.

Chapter 6: 23 Questions

STATS

This chapter covers several Porsche model types

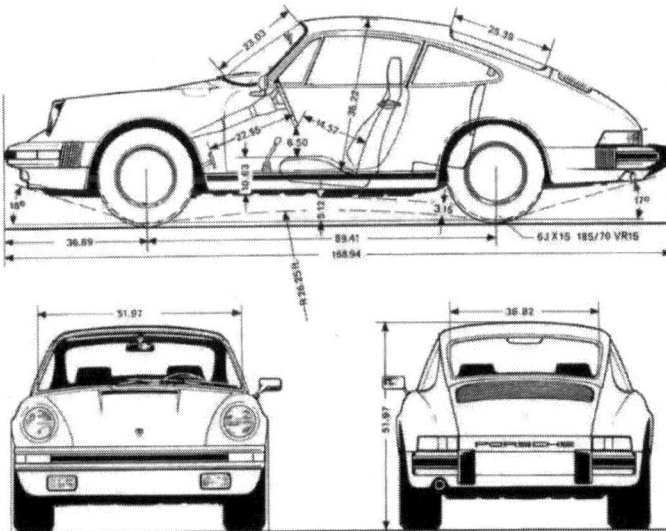

1. The 1973 5.4-liter 917/30 had power in excess off

e. 800 bhp
f. 900 bhp
g. 1000 bhp
h. 1100 bhp

2. The internal code numbers for 911s from 1989 until 2022 are generally as follows – 964, 993, 996, 997, 991, 992

a. True
b. False

3. In 1978 Porsche revised the 930 with a
_____engine which produced 300 bhp

a. 3.1 liter
b. 3.2 liter
c. 3.3 liter
d. 3.4 liter

4. The 964 was the second car in the world to offer dual airbags as standard. The firs being the 1987 Porsche 944 Turbo.

a. True
b. False

5. In 1976 'Moby Dick' was the nickname of the

a. 930
b. 935
c. 917
d. An adult performance act in Hamburg

6. In 1983 Stefan Bellof established a record time that would stand for 35 years for lapping the Nürburgring Nordschcleife in 6:11:13 during qualifying. He was driving a

a. 911
b. Citroen 2CV
c. 956
d. 963

7. This 35-year-old record was finally beaten by Timo Bernard in a derestricted Porsche 919 Evo on 29th June 2018

a. True
b. False

8. Who was Chief Designer at Porsche from 1931 to 1965?

a. Karl Rabe
b. Ferdinand Porsche
c. Ferdinand Piech
d. Erwin Komenda

9. Franz Xaver Reimspiess invented the Volkswagen logo and filed over 10 patents for his inventions used on Porsche engines and independent wheel/suspension systems

a. True
b. False

10. Ferdinand Porsches son Ferry and Robert Eberan Von Eberhorst worked on 'project 356' together in an old sawmill in Gmund in

a.1945
b.1946
c.1947
d.1948

11. All 911s including special editions had air-cooled engines up until

a. 1993
b 1995
c.1997
d.1999

12.The 2021 911 Turbo S gets from 0-60 mph in.

a. 5.6 seconds

b. 4.3 seconds

c. 3.8 seconds

d. 2.6 seconds

13. The Weissach masterpiece that is the 991 GT2 RS has

a. 650 bhp

b. 670 bhp

c. 700 bhp

d. 720 bhp

14. GT stands for Gran Turismo on the Porsche GT models

a. True

b. False

15. 911 GT2s are rear wheel drive apart from the GT2 RS

a. True

b. False

16.   Porsche is the largest manufacturer of racing cars in the world

a. True

b. False

17. The 993 Turbo was the first production Porsche 911 AWD Turbo model

a. True

b. False

18. The 993 Turbo S has a top speed of

a. 188 mph

b. 178 mph

c. 167 mph

d. 157 mph

19. The X50 package on the 996 Turbo upped power to 414 hp

a. True

b. False

20. The 991 Speedsters carbon fiber composite bonnet is 2KG lighter than that on the GT3

a. True
b. False

21. Porsche first experimented with active rear wheel steering on the

a. 918 Spyder
b. 991 GT3
c. 928
d. 987.2 Boxster Spyder

22. The 911 was once described as a 'practical supercar' because it had 4 seats and could return 30mpg on a run.

a. True
b. False

23. The 930 was the first 911 to be dubbed the

a. Haymaker
b. Bed maker
c. Widow maker
d. Marriage wrecker

Chapter 6: AnsweRS

1. c. 1000 bhp
2. a. True
3. c. 3.3 liter
4. a. True
5. b. 935
6. c. 956
7. a. True
8. a. Karl Rabe
9. a. True
10. c.1947
11. c.1997
12. d. 2.6 seconds
13. c. 700 bhp
14. a. True
15. b. False all GT2s are rear wheel drive
16. a. True
17. a. True
18. a. 188 mph
19. b. False it was 444 hp
20. a. True
21. c. 928
22. a. True
23. c. Widow maker

Fast facts

- The current most expensive Porsche to date is the Porsche 917 K bearing the number 917 – 024. It sold for over $14 million.

- At speeds of 200 mph the Porsche 956 racecar could theoretically drive on the ceiling due to the laws of speed.

- With over 1100 bhp and speeds of up to 240 mph the Porsche 917 from the early 1970s could still beat many modern race cars.

- Porsche has won several awards for its designs of Linde Material Handling forklifts.

- When Porsche adjusted the 993 during 1994-1997 to meet environmental laws for the US market, Sweden kept the original European model.

- Each 911 sun visor has 200 hand stiches and takes 45 mins to complete.

Chapter 7: 20 Questions

POPULAR CULTURE

2014 type 991

1. Which model of Porsche is Sally Carrera from the Cars movie?

a. 1999 911 type 996
b. Carrera GT
c. 2005 911 type 997
d. 2002 911 type 996

2. The 1969 movie Downhill Racer starred Robert Redford in a yellow_____

a. 1969 911E
b. 1968 911T
c. 1967 911R
d. 1968 911S

3. The 1971 Movie Le Mans starring Steve McQueen featured a 1970 911S

a. True
b. False

4. The 1984 movie Against All Odds Jeff Bridges is seen driving a _____in a race against James Woods in a Ferrari 308

a. 1983 911SC Cabriolet
b. 1983 911SC Targa
c. 1983 911 Turbo Convertible
d. 1983 911 Slant nose

5. The 1985 movie Commando starring Arnold Schwarzenegger features a known 'movie blooper' involving what type of 911?

a.1969 911 Targa
b. 1984 930
c. 1983 911SC Targa
d. 1972 911 Targa

6. The movie Weird Science in 1985 shows Gary in a Ferrari Mondial QV Cabriolet and Wyatt in a black 911 Turbo.

a. True
b. False

7. In the 1983 movie Risky Business Tom Cruise crashes his dads 1979 911 into a lake.

a. True
b. False

8. When Charlie Sheen and DB Sweeny happen upon a gorgeous Ferrari 512 Boxer on Rodeo Drive in Beverly Hills in the 1987 movie No Man's Land, Sheen derides the car as?

a. A piece of crap
b. Italian trash
c. A money pit
d. All show – no blow

9. The rare 964 3.6 Turbo in the 1995 movie Bad Boys wore French number plates and was owned by the film's producer Michael Bay.

a. True
b. False

10. In the 2017 movie Atomic Blond James McAvoy drives a 1989 US spec 964 Turbo

a. True
b. False

11. In the movie Gone in 60 Seconds from 2000 a 1978 911 was rebodied to look like a 1999 911 type 996.

a. True
b. False

12. Which 911 had a corpse locked in the trunk in the movie The Dream Machine from 1991?

a. 1989 911 Carrera Cabriolet
b. 1990 911 Targa
c. 1973 2.7 RS
d. 1982 911 SC Cabriolet

13. In the movie Scarface from 1983 Tony Montana played by Al Pacino buys a brand new 911 Turbo

a. True
b. False

14. In the 1999 movie Office Space Garry Cole drives his blue _____ into the same parking space every day

a. 964
b. 993
c. 1982 911 SC
d. 996

15. The 2001 GT3 RS used in the movie Fast Five from 2011 was in reality a _____ with stickers and new wheels

a. 996 C2
b. 996 C4S
c. 996 GT3
d. 996 GT2

16. The 1981 movie Condorman with Michael Crawford had a series of black _____ and two 911s

a. 930s
b. 935s
c. 928s
d. 962s

17. Kelly McGillis drives a Porsche _____in the 1986 movie Top Gun

a. 911 Convertible
b. 356 Roadster
c. 911 Turbo
d. 928

18. The 2013 movie Red 2 starring Bruce Willis featured a black

a. 997 GTS
b. 997 C4S
c. 997 Turbo
d. 997 S

19. In the 2020 movie Bad Boys for Life Will Smith drives a_____?

a. 964 3.6 Turbo S
b. Robin Reliant
c. 992 C4S
d. Fiat 500

20. James Dean was a driving his Porsche 550 Spyder when he had a fatal collision. He could see the oncoming car.

a. True
b. False

21. Which hugely talented and famously modest author writes the best, most informative and entertaining Porsche books?

a. Bobby Dazzler
b. Fanny Schmeller
c. Robert McGowan ☺
d. Joe King

Chapter 7: Answers

1. d. 2002 911 type 996
2. b. 1968 911T
3. a. True
4. a. 1983 911SC Cabriolet
5. a. 1969 911 Targa
6. b. False – it was a 928
7. b. False – it was a 928 again!
8. b. Italian trash
9. a. True
10. a. True
11. a. True
12. a. 1989 911 Carrera Cabriolet
13. b. False – guess what? It was a 928!
14. c. 1982 911 SC
15. a. 996 C2
16. b. 935
17. b. 356 Roadster
18. a. 997 GTS
19. C. 992 C4S
20. a. True
21. b. Fanny Schmeller – No wait it's c. Robert McGowan!

Fast facts

- Actor Keanu Reeves black 993 C4 was stolen while he was filming. (This car often mis quoted as being a C4S).

- All Ferraris featured in the 1971 movie Le Mans were borrowed from a local distributer since Enzo Ferrari had previously refused due to the Porsche victory at the end.

- Each Porsche boxer engine takes 4.5 hours to assemble

- Singer Janis Joplin owned a psychcidelic 356 which sold for auction for $1.75 million in 2015.

- Porsche designed a car for F-1 called the 360 Cisitalia. It had 385 bhp and could to 200 mph. It never raced due to the owner's lack of funding and a change in the rules.

Chapter 8: 31 Questions

AWARDS & VICTORIES

2022 GT3 Cup Car

1. The 917 gave Porsche its first Le Mans victory in 1970

a. True
b. False

2. How many times did Porches racing team from Stuttgart win the Targa Florio?

a. 9
b. 10
c. 11
d. 12

3. The Targa Florio closed as a national sports car event due to safety reasons in

a. 1969

b. 1970

c. 1977

d. 1979

4. The 911 derived 935 Turbo won the 24 Hours of Le Mans in 1979

a. True

b. False

5. Porsche won the World Championship for Makes with 911 derived models in 1971, 1972, 1973 and 1974

a. True

b. False

6. Which 911 won world championship races in the mid 70's including Targa Florio and 24 Hours of Daytona?

a. 911 Carrera RSR
b. 911 R
C. 930
d. 911 CS

7. The 550A was affectionately known as the

a. Giant Slayer
b. Road Rocket
c. Little B'stard
d. Little shit

8. How many 997.2 GT3 RS 4.0 were made?

a. 300
b. 400
c. 500
d. 600

9. It took 2 years for the 911 to make its way into the 24 Hours of Le Mans

a. True
b. False

10. The Targa Florio winning 906 prototype was also known as the Carrera 6

a. True
b. False

11. Four prototypes of the 911 R were built in 1966

a. True
b. False

12. The 2.7 RS was the first 911 to sport the Carrera badge that initially appeared on the most powerful

a. 904s
b. 356s
c. Type 64s
d. 718 Spyders

13. How many times did Porsche have 1st class wins the Carrera Panamericana?

a. 11

b. 21

c. 2

d. 1

14. i - How many Porsches entered the 1953 Carrera Panamericana?

a. 3

b.4

c.5

d.6

ii – Which type were they?

a. 356C

b. 550

c. 962

d. 917

15. Which model was Porsches first homologation special?

a. 930
b. 550 Spyder
c. 2.7 RS
d. 718 RS

16. The next 911 RS after the 2.7 would be the type

a. 964 RS
b. 993 RS
c. G series RS
d. 996 RS

17. The 993 RS is 300lbs lighter than the last of the 991 GT3 RSs

a. True
b. False

18. How many 993 RSs were made?

a. 1104
b. 2003
c. 3010
d. 4000

19. The first GT2s was built to compete in the GT2 Class Racing and were badged as GT2.

a. True
b. False

20. The 997 GT2 RS is 70 kg lighter than the 997 GT2

a. True
b. False

21. For the 1974 IROC Championship 1973 Carrera RSR models had the ducktail spoiler removed and were fitted with a flat whale tail

a. True
b. False

22. At the time of writing which motorsport event has Porsche never won? (no choices offered – have a go!)

23. Porsche was the first manufacturer to have three of which?

a. Plug in hybrid models
b. Seatbelt points
c. Le Mans 24-hour race winners
d. All of the above

24. Porsche holds the record for most wins at the 24 Hours of Le Mans

a. True
b. False

25. How many class wins had Porsche had at the 24 Hours of Le Mans?

a. 105
b. 106
c. 107
d. 108

26. The Porsche 962 C first entered into competition in the _____ IMSA Championship in the US

a. 1972
b. 1979
c. 1982
d. 1984

27. What was the first official Porsche racing entrant?

a. 930
b. 356 SL
c. 550 Spyder
d. 962

28. in 1964 Porsche won its fifth Targa Florio victory in

a. 904
b. 911 RSR
c. 911 Turbo
d. 917

29. In 1999 the 911 was placed _____ in the Global Automotive Elections Foundations Car of the Century Competition

a. first
b. tenth
c. third
d. fifth

30. Sportscar international named the 911 number 5 in the list of Top Sportscars of the 1960's

a. True
b. False

31. The Carrera RS was number 7 on the list of Sportscars form the 70's

a. True
b. False

Chapter 9: Answers

1. a. True
2. c. 11
3. c. 1977
4. a. True
5. b. False it was 1976, '77, '78 and 1979
6. a. 911 Carrera RSR
7. a. Giant Slayer
8. d. 600
9. b. False – it took 3 years
10. a. True
11. b. False they were built in 1967
12. b. 356s
13. c. 2
14. i. b 4

    ii b 550
15. c. 2.7 RS
16. a. 964 RS
17. a. True
18. a. 1104
19. b. False – it was badged as GT
20. a. True
21. a. True

22. Formula 1
23. a. Plug in hybrid models
24. a. True
25. d. 108
26. d. 1984
27. b. 356 SL
28. a. 904
29. d. fifth
30. b. False – it was named number 3
31. a. True

Fast facts

- Porsche has competed in and won over 30,000 different events in a number of speed racing categories.

- The unforgettable Sabine Schmitz and Klaus Abbelen the founders of Frikadelli-Racing also competed und the Manthey Racing banner as part of their joint racing at the Nordschleife.

- As per question no. 29 the 911 came in 5th place for the Car of The Century Award on

18th December 1999. The VW Beetle was forth. The Ford Model T won.

- The 911 has one of the longest running nameplates in history.

- Porsche Carrera Cup GB entered its 19th year in 2021. With over 300 races to its name, it is the fastest single marque GT racing championship in the UK.

A Final Note

Well, we have come to the end. It always feels a little bit strange when a good book comes to an end does it not? As you may know by now, I am a lifelong Porsche enthusiast. I can talk about Porsches all day long and as such I want our discussion to continue. Part of the 911s magic is because at its core it was and remains unorthodox due to its rear mounted flat six boxer engine. Nothing else looks like it or drives like it. And because of this nothing else gets under your skin in quite the same way. If you've never driven one then give it a go. I think you will be impressed.

We've delved into a lot of Porsche 911 details and facts throughout this little book. With such an interesting and broad topic, one could easily branch off and form thought provoking questions on many different aspects of the wonderful 911 and the Porsche company. I hope I have chosen the type of questions and shared facts in this book that have tested your knowledge in an entertaining way and at the same time inspired you to want to learn more.

If have enjoyed my Porsche 911 trivia book it would mean a lot if you could please leave an honest review.

It is also my sincere hope that you are either planning on buying your first Porsche or adding another to the stable. Now is the time!

You can find me on Amazon, Goodreads, Instagram, the Facebook group Practically Free Porsche, and on my website www.starbunker.com

Thank you – and happy driving!

Robert McGowan.

berto1101@hotmail.co.uk

Printed in Great Britain
by Amazon

19730913R00063